Deeper Simplicity, Broader Generosity
Images of Financial Wholeness

By Celeste A. Ventura

Morehouse Publishing
NEW YORK

Morehouse Publishing, 4785 Linglestown Road, Suite 101, Harrisburg, PA 17112

Morehouse Publishing, 19 East 34th Street, New York, NY 10016

Morehouse Publishing is an imprint of Church Publishing Incorporated.

www.churchpublishing.org

Cover design: Laurie Klein Westhafer

Interior design and production: Helen H. Harrison

Cover photo and pages 112 and 115: The Right Reverend Mary Gray-Reeves at the Sea of Galilee/Lake Gennesaret

Photos on pages 12, 15, 25, 28, 40, 43, 56, 59, 64, 67, 72, 76, 80, 83, 88, 91, 96, 100, 104, 107 courtesy of ThinkStock.com. Used by permission.

Photos on pages 16, 19, 32, 36, 48, 52 © Celeste A. Ventura

Library of Congress Cataloging-in-Publication Data
A catalog record of this book is available from the Library of Congress

ISBN 13: 978-0-8192-3195-6 (pbk)

ISBN 13: 978-0-8192-3196-3 (ebook)

Printed in the United States of America

"*Celeste Ventura provides a much needed reflection on how spiritual and practical matters are brought together in our lives and the pathway of faith. Our living will be more hopeful and fulfilled when we connect our financial resources with the values and beliefs that are at the core of faith.* Deeper Simplicity, Broader Generosity *provides map and method to help us do that.*"

—The Reverend Dr. James B. Lemler, Rector, Christ Church, Greenwich, Connecticut

"*Through an offering of the rich imagery found in nature, the words of scripture and the stories of friends and family, this little book provides nourishing soil for the reader to discover their own story of values, needs, and gifts. With Celeste, one is able to ponder deeply the role of money in our lives, using that important gift to tell our story through our choices, our planning, and our gifts. It is a beautiful tool by which one may reflect deeply on stewardship.*"

—The Right Reverend Mary Gray-Reeves, Episcopal Diocese of El Camino Real

"*Soulful images. Biblical and religious truths. Personal stories. Distilled wisdom. Evocative questions for reflection. With the mind of a seasoned financial planner and the heart of a spiritual companion, Celeste Ventura has put together a practical, accessible guide for claiming our core values and living as if how we save, spend, invest, and gift our money really matters.*"

—Diane Stephens Hogue, Spiritual Faculty of Presbyterian CREDO and Affiliate Faculty of Spiritual Formation at Garrett-Evangelical Theological Seminary

"*This is a tremendous resource for anyone who wants to make a meaningful shift in aligning their spiritual lives with their financial lives. The power of this book lies in the invitation to explore and play with images that speak to the soul—the place where transformation incubates and takes hold.*"

> —The Reverend Laurel Johnston, Stewardship Officer (2008-2013), The Episcopal Church and Director of Alumni Affairs and Major Gift Officer, Church Divinity School of the Pacific

"*The use of stories is the perfect way for those who don't love numbers to become engaged in finding answers to solve their financial challenges. Each chapter brings a new insight.*"

> —The Reverend Rod Sewell, Educational Specialist, The Board of Pensions of the Presbyterian Church (USA)

"Deeper Simplicity, Broader Generosity *is a clearly-written gift of a book. It offers a set of enduring images that can move individuals and groups to see financial well-being in a new light. Many of these images are quite powerful, pushing and pulling us to consider how aligned our treasure is with our deepest values, long after turning the last page.*"

> —Miguel Angel Escobar, Senior Program Director, Episcopal Church Foundation

"'Give with meaning and passion and receive with deep gratitude, grace and somehow, some way, put the gift to use for the good of all.' Celeste Ventura's own words summarize well not only the theme of her book, but her life as well. She approaches the subject of finances in an authentic, transparent, and knowledgeable way that is engaging and accessible for all who seek to be faithful with the gifts God has given them."

—The Reverend Sharon K. Youngs, Pastor of First Presbyterian Church, Oak Ridge, Tennessee

❧ *Dedication* ❧

*T*o all participants, staff, and faculty of the wider intentional learning community, known as CREDO (Clergy Reflection, Education, Discernment Opportunity) throughout The Episcopal Church and the Presbyterian Church (PCUSA). I am grateful our paths have crossed. You have fed my soul and enriched my life. May the fruit of our time together continue to break boundaries, cross borders, enrich and transform the lives of many, and enhance the common good—here, there, and everywhere. ❧

❧ General Guidance ❧

This book is intended as general guidance and is not financial advice. This book is merely intended for personal or congregational study regarding how one can build financial knowledge through a lens of faith. We accept no liability for any loss or damage whatsoever arising as a consequence of any use of or the inability to use any information contained in this book and you agree to indemnify and hold Church Publishing Incorporated and the author harmless for your use of the information contained in this book. Individuals and congregations are strongly urged to be in contact with their financial advisor. ❧

✑ Contents ✑

❧ *Acknowledgements* ❧

I am deeply grateful for the impressive guidance, wisdom, patience, and knowledge of Sharon Pearson at Church Publishing. Working with her through the development and editing of this book has been a gift and an experience of joy that I will long treasure. Robin Lybeck's skill, especially with photos and design, technical knowledge and communication was invaluable. Muchas Gracias to all at Church Publishing.

For fellow laity and clergy in the Diocese of El Camino Real and particularly fellow parishioners and clergy at St. Mary's by-the-Sea: our common pathways have nurtured and inspired me. For those with whom I have shared the experience of Education for Ministry, the experience of formation has been invaluable.

For friends near and far: our times of laughter and sorrow, our shared history, our shared adventures, whether they be in or along oceans, hiking mountain trails, or walking through medieval towns and castles, have helped to shape and model the person I wish to be when I grow up.

May our lives, service, words, and engagement embody the words of Archbishop Desmond Tutu, channeling Martin Luther King Jr. on the election of Barack Obama as the 44th President of the United States of America:

> *We are all caught up in a delicate network of interdependence, unable to celebrate fully our own heritage and place in the world, unable to realize our full potential as human beings, unless everyone else, everywhere else, can do the same.* — *Archbishop Desmond Tutu*[1]

∽ *Introduction* ∽

Whenever one contemplates, one necessarily at the same time contemplates in images.

Aristotle[2]

I invite you, daily over the coming week, to complete the sentence: The Kingdom of God is like . . . .

As you do so, wonder, ponder, and consider the underlining deep meaning and truth held by the associated images in your mind. Name those images, draw those images, and reflect on those images. Are your finances within or without the images? Do they reflect the Kingdom of God?

Or as Aristotle's words have been summarized for well over a millennium, "The soul never thinks without a picture."

Circa four hundred years later, Jesus did not speak about sheep and vineyards because he wanted the people to become better shepherds and superb wine makers. Wanting to transform lives, he used a variety of then thoroughly understood first-century images, analogies, and parables to teach, to guide, and to change hearts. He did it well and there is no reason for us not to take his lead. After all, as people rooted in the biblical story, we are usually very comfortable in the world of reflection and are quite conversant in using images, analogies, and story to reveal a message, a

> *The soul never thinks without a picture.*

pathway—a deeper truth. To put it in simple sacramental language, we are people of outward and visible signs.

Images can be entrees to our understanding of new concepts and often have a universal aspect. They help us break boundaries and cross borders. If you have ever felt restricted in trying to understand financial matters or arrived at borders that block addressing and managing your finances, seeing finances through a lens of images is a pathway you might want to journey.

Images can be entrees to our understanding of new concepts.

At the beginning of each of the chapters that follow, you will discover an image—some will be familiar, others might, at first, puzzle you. As you read my reflections following each visual cue, I invite you to follow your path of discovery toward financial wholeness.

What are the pathways in your financial vision? Are they complicated or simple? Do they generate worry, or are they open and full of rich soil for growth? Over the past six years, the phrase "deeper simplicity, broader generosity" has been a visual pathway for me as I deal with and plan the financial threads of my life. I gleaned it from a 2009 pastoral letter from the House of Bishops (Episcopal) in which they encouraged the Church to rise above fear and offer hope, to reach out to those suffering from loneliness and anxiety, and to share our resources with one another. This book seeks to help us become financially whole, spiritually as well as wise stewards of our money, offering ways to explore deeper simplicity and broad generosity. I encourage you to consider adding it as a thread in your life journey as I have in mine.

To help guide your individual time of reflection or your group's discussion, each chapter concludes with several reflection questions. As you ponder the practical as well as the conceptual, the images presented and stories told, think about your own financial wholeness. What are the new patterns of behavior God is calling you to follow? How are your core values reflected in your handling of finances? What refinements need to be made? ∾

∞ 1 ∞

The Importance of a Trellis

When you gather the grapes of your vineyard,
do not glean what is left; it shall be for the alien,
the orphan, and the widow.
Deuteronomy 24:21

A few years back, a group of us gathered in the wine
country of Northern California to celebrate the
thirtieth birthday of a dear friend's youngest daughter. It
was a memory-making, enlightening, and grand celebration.

One afternoon, as we were walking
through a vineyard and were surrounded
by lush, green, healthy vines, I realized
my technical knowledge of how grapes
are grown was surprisingly and embarrassingly limited. The aha was that only
some vines would bear fruit . . . others
would not; vines growing along banks of
the hills along the trail, as gorgeous as they were, would
not bear fruit, while those with the support of a trellis
have the opportunity to be quite fruitful.

> *What are the pieces I need to build my trellis to produce this fruit?*

All the vines had the same environment: cool nights, rich soil, proper watering, pruning, and sun—yet without a trellis, no fruit. A trellis is essential to support and guide growth, allow air to circulate, and most importantly to expose the vine to full sunlight . . . and yes, this also relates to finances.

Practices such as budgeting, financial planning, saving, patience, dialogue, and wise investing provide the cool nights, rich soil, watering, and pruning, while thoughtful development of core values, awareness of passion, vision, a Rule of Life, and openness to change provide a flexible trellis.

> *A trellis is essential to support and guide growth.*

A trellis for a vineyard requires a series of wires, braces, and wooden posts. The structure, although adaptable over time and changing conditions, must have longevity, including the ability to withstand harsh weather, brutal wind, and long periods of heat. The structure needs to be deeply anchored in the ground so as not to topple with every slight shift in the soil.

Components for your financial trellis—the wires, braces, and posts that support your financial picture—are a result of reflection on and discernment of your priorities.

Ask yourself along with significant others in your life, "What is the fruit I wish my handling of finance matters could produce?" "What are the pieces I need to build my trellis to produce this fruit . . . what light and air and grace and hope and love can I weave together to bring it forth?" Form this discernment into a group of core values and spiritual practices, then weave them in your Rule of Life to guide you in showing forth God's light and *ruach*—wind, spirit, and breath. In other words, fruitful financial planning is a matter of both heart and mind, practical and conceptual—both/and not either/or. ॐ

᪥ Reflection Questions ᪥

1 Read Deuteronomy 24:19–22. Much of this fifth book of the Hebrew Scriptures aims to provide the framework for a covenant between Israel and God. It invites God's people to have an awareness of the obligations each individual has toward God and one another. What does this passage mean to you in the context of your life today?

_____

_____

_____

_____

_____

_____

_____

_____

_____

_____

_____

_____

_____

_____

2 What are the components of your financial trellis?

_____

_____

_____

_____

_____

_____

_____

_____

_____

_____

_____

_____

_____

_____

_____

_____

_____

_____

3 What is the anchor that holds your "trellis" in place?

_____

_____

_____

_____

_____

_____

_____

_____

_____

_____

_____

_____

_____

_____

_____

_____

_____

_____

4 What are your core values and how can you apply
them to your financial planning?

_____

_____

_____

_____

_____

_____

_____

_____

_____

_____

_____

_____

_____

_____

_____

_____

_____

2

Jack Pines and Artichokes

Jack Pines . . . are not lumber trees (and they) won't win many beauty contests either. But to me this valiant old tree, solitary to its own rocky point, is as beautiful as a living thing can be. . . . In the calligraphy of its shape against the sky is written strength of character and perseverance, survival of wind, drought, cold, heat, disease. . . . In its silence it speaks of . . . wholeness . . . an integrity that comes from being what you are.

Douglas Wood[3]

Parker Palmer, in *A Hidden Wholeness*,[4] begins his first chapter, "Images of Integrity," with this quote from Douglas Wood, a Minnesotan whose wilderness is different than my wilderness. As Dr. Palmer uses the words "wholeness" and "undivided" to define integrity, I wonder how and where integrity has been manifested in my life. When have I felt wholeness, and did the feeling last? If it did not last, does that make the experience

> *I wonder where integrity has been manifested in my life.*

of wholeness for a while any less whole? What were the joys associated with feeling whole and living into, as John Donne states, being "part of the main?"[5]

I also began to explore specific times when, on hindsight, integrity was clearly manifested in the lives of others. How might our financial planning, our saving, investing, and sharing contribute to wholeness?

I recognize that outward and visible signs assist me greatly as I grapple with integrity in my financial life and so I, a person integrally part of coastal California, began to wonder what is an image of integrity for me. What is the image of someone who perseveres and survives the environment—both the internal and external environment—and yet emerges being true to what and who they are? The image that often recurs for me is that of an artichoke.

How might our financial planning contribute to wholeness?

Agricultural families in my greater geographic area have grown artichokes for centuries. You can see field after field of them along our rolling coastal farmland. In the spring, their beautiful soft purple blooms rise up and catch your eye. However, when harvested, the leaves are tough and cracked, with prickly tips that can draw blood, while the stem is worn, dirty, and beginning to fall apart. The artichoke itself does not evoke the word *beauty*; it is not perfection. It is, like Douglas Wood's jack pine, what it is: a budding, blooming, then course and barely edible thistle—an image of wholeness, of integrity.

As I use the artichoke, Parker Palmer uses the jack pine image as a way to begin exploring what it means to be whole, what it means to have integrity. In his words integrity "means embracing brokenness as an integral part of life . . . devastation can be used as a seedbed for a new life."[6] The opposite is a divided life, when our lives become separated from our bedrock, from our soul, from God's image in which we were created. Palmer's first chapter is particularly intriguing as it offers an opportunity to explore integrity in all facets of our lives.

What is an image or who is a model of integrity for you? Who in your life has modeled wholeness in choosing to use their gifts for the benefit of the common good over self-interest? Recount the stories behind the actions they took. Take some time to reflect. Two or three images might come to mind. For now choose one and give some thought to how this image is reflected, or not, in your financial life.

The heart is the soul of an artichoke, the desired entity that was your quest.

I return to the image of an artichoke in reflecting on integrity and my financial life. To prepare the artichoke for eating, one must tear off the dry crispy leaves, cut away the prickly pointy tips, and trim the stem. You drop the artichokes in seasoned boiling water along with a sufficient amount of olive oil, and you let the transformation begin. Once tender, you can enjoy a taste of the "meat" of the leaves and then discard them. They have served their purpose by protecting the heart of the artichoke. The heart is the soul of an artichoke, the desired entity that was your quest.

Handling our finances requires much of the same, with one exception. To stay true to who we are, we peel off old ways, ways that are no longer working for us. We are to discard ways that are prickly—ways that prevent us from being who we are, who God created us to be. Unlike the jack pine and the artichoke, however, we have the gift, or a curse as Parker Palmer states, of choice. Taking the road less traveled, the road of integrity, means making a choice to, as Palmer writes, "refuse to live a divided life."[7] I encourage you to choose wholeness, not perfection in your financial dealings—to choose "an integrity that comes from being what you are."[8] ℃

⚜ Reflection Questions ⚜

1 Read the quote from Douglas Wood that begins this essay. What words stand out for you?

_____

_____

_____

_____

_____

_____

2 What does integrity mean to you? What images are associated with this?

_____

_____

_____

_____

_____

_____

_____

_____

3 Have you ever noticed a disconnection, dividedness, between how you plan to handle your finances, the reality of your situation, and how you actually live into your financial plans? List some of these instances.

_____

_____

_____

_____

_____

_____

_____

_____

_____

_____

_____

_____

_____

_____

4 Is my legacy, as reflected in my financial plan and action, congruent with, and integrally a part of, the wholeness of God's dream? If not, how can I begin to move in this direction?

_____

_____

_____

_____

_____

_____

_____

_____

_____

_____

_____

_____

_____

_____

_____

_____

❦3❦
Shaping Your Wildness

He removes every branch in me that bears no fruit.
Every branch that bears fruit he prunes
to make it bear more fruit.

John 15:2

During my childhood, Charlie and Lucille lived up the street. Every time I walked through their gate, I was fascinated by their Japanese-style garden. It was a work of art, and even at my young age, I understood the effort and care it took to keep it that way. Charlie raked the sand on a daily basis; rocks and pools of water were strategically placed as were what looked like miniature trees and bushes. Bamboo framed the area, and a mound of moss, about three or four feet high, was impeccably manicured. As I grew older I understood the mound to represent Mount Fuji, the trees to be bonsai, and the garden itself to be reflective of Charlie's wonderful memories and deep appreciation for the culture and people of Japan where, pre-World War I, he had lived as a young boy.

> *It was a work of art, and even at my young age, I understood the effort and care it took to keep it that way.*

Bonsai, an ancient Chinese art form, began over a thousand years ago and migrated from China to Japan as well as to other cultures. When carefully shaped and nurtured, bonsai trees can live for more than one hundred years, and many reach slightly over three feet tall. Those who practice bonsai speak of the meditative, reflective aspect of their art and of a deep connection to nature.

Recently, while attending a conference, I was fascinated to see someone practicing the art of bonsai on a tall, wild black oak growing on a knoll on the grounds of the Chapel Rock Conference Center near Prescott, Arizona. It was during Sabbath time on Sunday, and this was his way of spending time in reflection, aware of and listening to the presence of God. Slowly, using large pruning shears, he shaped the oak, stepping back with every cut to see and consider what was emerging. Paraphrasing what Michelangelo is believed to have said long ago, he saw a work of art in the wildness of a very unkempt tree and set it free. The messy tangle of branches and leaves that we walked by many times each day emerged as a creative form—its true self revealed and a delight for our eyes.

The messy tangle of branches and leaves emerged as a creative form, its true self revealed and a delight for our eyes.

Once home, I began to wonder if the image of shaping the tall, wild black oak might be a useful one to consider as we shape our financial pathways. I imagine there has been and will be, for each of us, a time when our finances seem to be a wild unkempt mess. Our natural inclination is to figuratively walk right on by, not even noticing the mess . . . and if we do notice, simply hoping it will go away. It won't.

Step back. Take a look at your finances. Is there a place where a little pruning is needed? If so, gently trim what might be restaurant meals or those new shoes you really do not need. Then step back again and appreciate what trimming reveals. Is there another area, maybe in the realm of gifts, where a practice of saving can be instated? How might you model gift giving for the next generation? Think of gifts given to children, godchildren, and grandchildren—yours or those of friends. What comes to mind, especially at birthdays and Christmas, is a bunch of toys and video games. I wonder what giving and receiving would be like if a third of the money was spent on a gift for the child, a third was given in honor of the child, and the final third might best be placed in a 529 College Fund for the child. This to me is a both/and decision, a both/and gift; it passes on a value, addresses needs, expresses care for the next generation, can be a sign of abundant life, and gives the child a present to open, a present to save, and a present given in their name. Who knows? As they grow older, they just might assume the practice as their own. The wild mess is once more being shaped, nurtured, and formed, revealing a new identity. In terms of psychoanalyst Erik Erikson's *Eight Stages of Psychosocial Development* (learning generativity versus self-absorption),[9] generativity is concern for and guidance of the next generation. How we shape our finances (and our children) is planted and established at an early age.

> *Take a look at your finances. Is there a place where a little pruning is needed?*

Is there an area in your financial life where many dollars are being spent in an effort to create memories and bring family closer together? If so, is there a simpler way to create memories and build bonds? A friend of mine shared what a special treat it was, when the temperature was over ninety degrees, to share a cup of frozen yogurt with his young daughter while they sat under an old elm tree. It is now a practice of theirs to do so at least once a week regardless of the weather—just the two of them.

It takes effort and care to shape our financial lives into a delight for the eyes, heart, and mind. Step back. Take a look. What do you see and what would you like to emerge? Are there ways you might prune and shape your financial life? How might your financial practices be a vehicle of generativity—a concern for establishing and guiding the next generation? You might want to consider keeping a journal of your thoughts, and/or share them with others as tools to begin putting them into practice. ∾

❧ *Reflection Questions* ❧

1 Read John 15:1–17. What does it mean to you to abide in Jesus? What fruit do you bear that will last?

_____

_____

_____

_____

_____

_____

_____

2 What is your financial "tall, wild black oak"?

_____

_____

_____

_____

_____

_____

_____

_____

3 Ask yourself, is my legacy, as reflected in my financial plan and action, congruent with, and integrally a part of, the wholeness of God's dream? If it isn't, what steps do you need to follow to move in this direction?

_____

_____

_____

_____

_____

_____

_____

_____

_____

_____

_____

_____

_____

_____

_____

4 How might one of the following agencies assist in your giving to others? Do you have a charity close to your heart?

_____

_____

_____

_____

_____

_____

_____

_____

_____

_____

ᕑ *Urban Promise Wellness Center* www.urbanpromiseusa. org/wellness-center

ᕑ *Nets for Life Inspiration Fund* www.episcopalrelief. org/church-in-action/church-campaigns/ netsforlife-inspiration-fund

ᕑ *Our Little Roses in Honduras* www.ourlittleroses.org

ᕑ Buy, through *Episcopal Relief and Development,* a goat or a pig for a family in need www.episcopalrelief. org

4

Giving and Receiving

For it is in giving that we receive.

St. Francis of Assisi

Decades ago, a few days after my grandmother's death, as my father and I were in her apartment, I saw a box on the top shelf of the kitchen cupboard. It looked familiar. I took it down, opened it, and found the electric mixer I gave her on Christmas, about eight years prior. It was still in its original box—unused. I can recall the feeling of disappointment and of wondering why she had not used it. Intellectually, however, I knew the gift was not appropriate. My grandmother was an immigrant from Italy. She arrived in her mid-teens, lived the next five decades of her life in Lower Manhattan's Little Italy and an Italian neighborhood in Jackson Heights. I could almost hear her saying, "Wooden spoons are all I need. Why bother with an electric mixer?" Strange, isn't it, how a slice of life, such as this, remains with us decades later?

Strange, isn't it, how a slice of life, such as this, remains with us decades later?

Have you ever specifically explored what events occurred, and what values were absorbed, in how your parents and grandparents handled money? Were there cultural influences to consider in their handling of money? The electric mixer could be a metaphor of legacy giving and receiving between today's world and that of my grandmother's, however a Maasai boy offers a more powerful global story.

In the aftermath of the 9/11 attacks, a Kenyan named Kimeli returned to his village from New York City with stories of this tragic event and ideas about of how he would like to help the Americans who were suffering. The story has been retold in *14 Cows for America*[10] and is described in *The New York Times* by Nicholas Kristof, entitled "Foreign Aid."[11] *14 Cows for America* is a reminder that everyone can make a difference. It is a story about the relationship between Kimeli, a young Maasai boy, his tribe, and America. It is a wonderful example of legacy, of giving and receiving, immersed in foundational values, passion, and compassion.

> *Give with meaning and passion and receive with deep gratitude and grace and ... put the gift to use for the good of all.*

For the Maasai, the giving of a cow, much less fourteen cows, is a gift of life. For the American ambassador and his wife (on the receiving end), it was a gift that touched them to their core. For both the Maasai and the Americans, this exchange has led to ongoing life (now thirty-four cows and counting), and is a reminder, paraphrasing a quote from the book: "There is no person so powerful she/he can not be touched by receiving a heartfelt, compassionate gift, nor a person so small or unknown that he/she can not give what is life to them."[12]

Forget trying to be appropriate, I told myself. Give with meaning and passion and receive with deep gratitude and grace, and somehow, some way, put the gift to use for the good of all. ∾

For the Maasai, the giving of a cow, much less fourteen cows, is a gift of life.

☞ *Reflection Questions* ☜

1 Read *A Prayer attributed to St. Francis* (the Book of Common Prayer, p. 833). How is giving rooted in receiving? What are the motives you have for giving to others?

_____

_____

_____

_____

_____

_____

_____

_____

_____

_____

_____

_____

_____

_____

2 What are the money messages that influence your handling of money?

_____

_____

_____

_____

_____

_____

_____

_____

_____

_____

_____

_____

_____

_____

_____

_____

_____

_____

3 Are there stories about giving and receiving that speak to you of deep meaning and lasting gratitude?

_____

_____

_____

_____

_____

_____

_____

_____

_____

_____

_____

_____

_____

_____

_____

_____

_____

4 If it were to be written today, what would your legacy of giving and receiving be?

_____

_____

_____

_____

_____

_____

5 What money messages are portrayed in your practice, and are there changes to be made?

_____

_____

_____

_____

_____

_____

_____

_____

_____

5

Pathways and Journeys

... where the pathway dies, the journey has begun.
Thomas Merton[13]

At times in my life this phrase has provided solace and has allowed me, albeit on occasion with fear and trepidation, and always cautiously, to seek the journey to come. A new journey makes itself evident and is usually in a form I had not previously considered. The more pathways have died and new journeys have begun, the more comfortable I am that a new journey will appear. Still the dying is rarely something I welcome.

Most of us, at sometime in our life, have had a pathway or, most likely, many pathways die. The death of a pathway can seem like falling off a cliff, whether it is a fiscal cliff or a relational, spiritual, vocational, or health cliff and usually involves strands of all facets of our lives.

> *The death of a pathway can seem like falling off a cliff.*

At other times pathways can seem smooth and almost mindless—something we take for granted, a known entity. If we look closely, those pathways can also be a source for reflection. If we are not paying attention, we will miss an opportunity. In reality, most pathways require non-linear discernment of steps: some large, some small, some sideways, some backwards, some steep. Many pathways can be loose and squishy as islands of wet sand. I call these pathways my "hop, skip, and jump" pathways—ones where I need to pay attention, not simply leisurely walk the familiar. Financial planning can, at times, be a "hop, skip, and jump" pathway.

> *Many pathways can be loose and squishy as islands of wet sand. I call these pathways my "hop, skip, and jump" pathways.*

Take a look at your financial situation. Where is your attention needed? What are the variety of twists and turns needed to navigate some wet and squishy sand? Following are some reminders of areas for you to establish sure footing.

Cash Management: Build savings to needed levels for what you see ahead and reduce debt to a manageable and wise level. For some, zero debt is a wise goal, and for others a reasonable, manageable mortgage, especially with today's historically low interest rates, may provide prudent leverage. Wise cash management increases the choices open to you in the future.

Insurance: Consider your, and in many cases your family's, particular situation. What needs to be covered? Does life insurance—either term or whole life—need to be increased or decreased or, in some cases, initiated? Try a life insurance calculator.[14] In addition, have you considered long-term care and/or health care costs during an approaching retirement?

Investments: Have you established a 403(b) or 401(k) retirement savings account? Have you reviewed your asset allocation, determined an appropriate allocation, and made necessary changes? It is wise to review, with a financial advisor, your allocation at least once a year. Remember, Social Security and a defined benefit pension are considered "bond-like," so you might want to consider some growth investments with your retirement funds.

Estate Planning: What is the legacy you are living? What will your family, friends, and community recognize as your legacy? What does generosity mean and how is it visible in your handling of financial matters? Have you completed the documentation, such as a will, a trust, a power of attorney for both financial and health matters, to make this so? If appropriate, are your guardianship papers for your minor children up-to-date?

> *What does generosity mean and how is it visible in your handling of financial matters?*

As you look ahead, what are the twists and turns of your financial pathway? To help you decide a pathway to take, consider the cyclical pathway created by CREDO[15] (Clergy Reflection, Education, Discernment Opportunity) for employees, both clergy and lay, of The Episcopal Church. This cyclical pathway, known as IDPT, encourages and leads us through a process of Identity, Discernment, Practice, and Transformation. At first glance, it seems to be a smooth pathway. You take one step, then another, and then another, and voilà—transformation. However we all know life does not unfold so smoothly . . . identity can change; discernment can leave us wondering whose wisdom we are seeking and if what we are hearing is really of God. Practice can go back and forth. We hop into one practice only to find it is not serving us well, so we jump onto another practice to test its viability. Somewhere along the way, we look back, then ahead, and realize transformation has occurred and we have a new identity. As Merton said in *Elias*, "The pathway has ended, the journey has begun."

⚬❧ *Reflection Questions* ☙⚬

1 Read Psalm 23. What are the paths God is guiding you to follow?

_____

_____

_____

_____

_____

_____

_____

_____

_____

_____

_____

_____

_____

_____

_____

_____

_____

2 What areas of financial footing do you need assistance for? Who might you turn to for help?

_____

_____

_____

_____

_____

_____

_____

3 Are you insured for those unexpected pathways that may arise in the future? If not, how might you begin that planning?

_____

_____

_____

_____

_____

_____

_____

4 Where have you seen transformation in your life: personally, spiritually, and even financially?

_____

_____

_____

_____

_____

_____

_____

5 How might you be more discerning of the paths you choose in your future?

_____

_____

_____

_____

_____

_____

_____

_____

∽6∾

From Another Perspective

*I only went out for a walk and finally
concluded to stay out till sundown, for going out,
I found, was really going in.*

John Muir[16]

Many of you will recognize this iconic view of Yosemite's Half Dome. It is seen from the valley floor and is similar to the view from the scenic outlooks on the southwest slopes that rise above Yosemite Valley. Logic would tell us there are many other ways to view Half Dome, yet for the most part, photographers and visitors gravitate to this well-known vista.

If you go deeper into Yosemite, you will see Half Dome from another perspective.

If you go deeper into Yosemite, up to Tuolumne Meadows and hike to Vogelsang High Sierra Camp,[17] at 10,100 feet you will have the opportunity to see Half Dome from another perspective. I find it an even more stunning view. Hike out of Tuolumne at a reasonable time in the morning, and you will be at Vogelsang by mid-afternoon, with plenty of time to settle into your tent cabin and have an early supper. Then go with a friend, a daypack, a warm vest, and a bottle of water, and climb up another five hundred feet or so to the slope of the west-facing ridge of Vogelsang Peak and wait. Come sunset, watch in awe as another perspective emerges—the backside of Half Dome. Far in the distance, enveloped in hues of gold and red, yellow and orange, creation in all her glory will seem to lie down and slumber, and you just might experience, in this alpine thin-place, a palpable awareness of God's presence.

For me the experience some twenty-six years ago this summer was absolutely glorious. The sunset was a mixture of red and orange hues intermixed with streaks of clouds in various shades of gray and white. I did not have a camera, but the image is embedded in my mind, on my heart. It is a view from another perspective.

You just might experience a palpable awareness of God's presence.

Like the iconic view of Half Dome, understanding our cash flow through the lens of income and expenses is one view, certainly a necessary view. However, it is not the only view. It is hard for the pragmatic list of numbers and line items to offer the nuance needed to punctuate and make palpable the depth of our passions, hopes, and dreams. What you need is a trellis (see chapter 1), formed by the conceptual.

What if our first step in budgeting was to create and weave together a narrative, a trellis, using a lens of core values, a Rule of Life, and/or a meaningful statement of how we strive to live our lives? Just as General Convention (or General Assembly, whatever your denominational polity) created and adopted The Episcopal Church's 2013–2015 and 2016–2018 budgets through the perspective of Five Marks of Mission,[18] we might think in a similar vein and name the beliefs, values, and passions that we wish to be visible in how we earn, save, share, and spend our money.

Have you ever thought of understanding your cash flow through a perspective other than the normal list of line items in a budget? As I have only dabbled in this idea myself, I am certainly not coming to this question with all the answers. Ponder what might be your process. Where is your dream of establishing a school in Cameroon? How is your passion for local produce and health education within an inner city visible in your budget spreadsheet? Are the ocean bays and inland waterways in need of your attention, and if so, how will that be funded? Where is your goal to contribute to the nurture and education of girls in Honduras or South Sudan?

Have you ever thought of understanding your cash flow through a perspective other than the line items in a budget?

Pose questions and wonder how your financial planning process might make palpable your trellis of hopes, passions, and dreams with supporting goals. ◌

❦ Reflection Questions ❦

1 Read the verses of the hymn "Amazing Grace" by John Newton (#671 in *The Hymnal 1982*). Have you ever been lost, then found? blind, then aware of a new perspective?

_____

_____

_____

_____

_____

_____

_____

_____

_____

_____

_____

_____

_____

_____

2 What are the beliefs, values, and passions that could serve as a lens in your budgeting?

_____

_____

_____

_____

_____

_____

_____

_____

_____

_____

_____

_____

_____

_____

_____

_____

3 Is there a portion of your budget that can be set aside for funding your passion?

_____

_____

_____

_____

_____

_____

_____

_____

_____

_____

_____

_____

_____

_____

_____

_____

4 What goals can you establish to begin to live out
your dreams?

_____

_____

_____

_____

_____

_____

_____

_____

_____

_____

_____

_____

_____

_____

_____

_____

_____

❧ 7 ❧

Deeper Simplicity, Broader Generosity

*In the beginning when God created the heavens
and the earth, the earth was a formless void and
darkness covered the face of the deep, while a
wind from God swept over the face of the waters.
Then God said, "Let there be light"; and there
was light. And God saw that the light was good;
and God separated the light from the darkness.
God called the light Day, and the darkness he
called Night. And there was evening and there
was morning, the first day.*

Genesis 1:1–5

ather's Day weekend is a grand weekend for parish
camp; it is doubly grand when you hear the opening
of Genesis among towering redwoods and
along a bubbling river. "And God saw that
it was good . . . and there was evening and
there was morning . . . ."

*And God saw
that it was good.*

The weather was delightful. Children were
laughing, rafting, and crafting. A grandpa
told stories around the campfire and a very content army

major, husband, father, and friend, on leave from Afghanistan, beer in hand, was in charge of the grill. New families met new friends. Memories were made. "And God saw that it was good . . . and there was evening and there was morning . . . ."

On Saturday, five of us went on a hike along the bluff and then up onto the coastal range ridge. As we began, a group of about fifteen young adults scampered past us. Their t-shirts sported *Crop Walk* and *AmeriCorps* logos. We quickly asked, and yes, they were part of a local AmeriCorps[19] group serving in a nearby agricultural community. Soon they were out of sight. We walked on. Hours passed. Suddenly there they were again, scampering up yet another hill to the shade of a grove of cypress trees. It was there that we joined them in a lengthy and fascinating conversation. They were from all over the country; recent college graduates, serving in a variety of ways. Some oversaw an after-school program, some organized a food bank, and others worked within the agricultural system to understand and, where possible, facilitate a better life for those laboring in the fields. You could sense the care and joy they had in each other's company. You could hear in their voice and enthusiasm the difference they were making. "And God saw that it was good and there was evening and there was morning . . . ."

> *You could sense the care and joy they had in each other's company.*

On reflection, driving home, I thought about these young people, the gift they give and the insight they receive. They were leading lives of "deeper simplicity and broader generosity." This phrase, gleaned from two separate comments, has stayed with me ever since I read the March 2009 pastoral letter, from the House of Bishops (Episcopal), regarding the financial crisis.[20] It spoke to rapidly increasing unemployment, declining home values with subsequent foreclosures, and decline in savings and investment. The letter, which continues to be powerful to this day, calls us to remember the struggles of our spiritual ancestors, their difficult journeys through the wildness, and their resilience as they found ways to simplify their lives and enhance their care for all of God's people. I found myself thinking: How can I live a life of deeper simplicity and broader generosity? What do I perceive to be the relationship between wealth or lack of wealth and identity? What is wealth? What roadblocks, such as trepidation, unease, and/or apprehensiveness, block my progress to live such a life? How can I journey into a deeper and broader undivided life, or, as Parker Palmer encourages us, to live a life of wholeness, blending simplicity and generosity into a life of integrity? "And God saw it was good . . . and there was evening and there was morning . . . ." ∿

> *How can I live a life of deeper simplicity and broader generosity?*

⁓ *Reflection Questions* ⁓

1 Read the account of creation in Genesis 1:1–31. What part of this story do you like best? Where are you in this story?

_____

_____

_____

_____

_____

_____

_____

_____

_____

_____

_____

_____

_____

_____

_____

2 Are there stories you can share about people who live lives infused with a deep simplicity and a broad generosity?

_____

_____

_____

_____

_____

_____

_____

_____

_____

_____

_____

_____

_____

_____

_____

3 Is leading a life of deeper simplicity, broader generosity, easier and more of a draw as we age, or does age make a difference?

_____

_____

_____

_____

_____

_____

_____

_____

_____

_____

_____

_____

_____

_____

_____

4 What impact, either helpful or harmful, do the economic realities of our times make on our ability to live such a life?

_____

_____

_____

_____

_____

_____

_____

_____

_____

_____

_____

_____

_____

_____

_____

_____

_____

_____

❧ 8 ❧

Water from Rock and Rock for Water

The Lord spoke to Moses, saying: Take the staff, and assemble the congregation, you and your brother Aaron, and command the rock before their eyes to yield its water. Thus you shall bring water out of the rock for them; thus you shall provide drink for the congregation and their livestock.

Numbers 20:7–8

In the summer of 2012, photos sent by friends on pilgrimage in the land of the Holy One seemed to come in on an almost daily basis. It was a delight to look for Jesus in the faces of the people, to see the prayers placed with hope between the stones of the Western Wall, and to recognize a multitude of familiar places from Scripture. At one point the pilgrims crossed the border into Jordan, traveling to Petra to experience the extraordinarily breathtaking "rose-red city half as old as time."[21]

> *It was a delight to look for Jesus in the faces of the people and to recognize a multitude of familiar places from Scripture.*

Petra, not far beyond the Jordan River, is the ancient home of the Nabataeans. It is a spectacular place I hope to explore some day. For now I am left to ponder the history of the place and the skill of the first century BCE Nabataeans, who were able to envision carving buildings into sandstone and making their vision a reality by raising up a magnificent community in a place where both drought and flash floods were common.

Archeologists help us understand how these desert people prepared for times of drought and protected themselves from the destructiveness of flash floods by diverting and storing water in times of flood so they could tap into it in times of drought. The taming of water, the diverting of water, the storing of water were essential to their survival. No wonder the Arab tradition holds that just northwest of Petra, in Wadi Musa, is the area where Moses struck a rock (*petra*) with his staff and water flowed.

The taming of water, the diverting of water, the storing of water were essential to their survival.

Using the Nabataeans' wise use and storage of water as an image, let's explore our own use and storage of money. The image has me pondering how best to live through times of financial drought and prepare financially for unexpected events, whether metaphorical or real flash floods, which rush into our lives. We do not have Moses's staff to strike the rock and make money flow; however, I do think there is a financial lesson to learn from these innovative ancient people.

Cash management, including setting aside money, is foundational to our financial health. The ancient community of Petra diverted water into cisterns. In this electronic era, with our household finances in mind, that might mean placing the amount needed for our monthly expenses in a checking or electronic bill-paying account, investing a portion, and allotting a portion for savings. Be innovative and disciplined, prepare for drought and flood, hopes and dreams.

Maybe your parents or grandparents used a system of placing cash in envelopes, each labeled for a particular need: emergency taxes, baby to be born, education, car repairs, wedding, retirement savings, vacation . . . you get the idea. Today, preparing can be facilitated by a variety of means. I would suggest creating a spreadsheet, preferably electronic, with columns (electronic cisterns, virtual envelopes) representing particular needs and hopes. Whatever the categories are for you, I would encourage you to consider adding a section for goals, whether those have been named or are yet to be named. You can create your own Excel spreadsheet or determine if some of the online budgeting tools available such as Mint.com or Quicken suit your needs.

Let us not forget, that there are communities where drought and flood are absolute realities, not metaphors.

Let us not forget, as our hearts remind us, that there are communities throughout the world where drought and flood are absolute realities, not metaphors. Whether we are lacking in water or money, or have an overabundance of either that can cause a detriment to the land as well as ourselves, I close with a portion of "For Water"[22]:

In the name of God, the Creator, whose wet breath breathed life into all living things, we pray about water.

We pray for places where, as in the days of Noah, water is too plentiful by flood, hurricane and storm surge.

We pray for places where water is too scarce as temperatures rise and droughts increase.

We pray for the women and children of today in many places in the world who must travel long distances for fresh water. Amen.

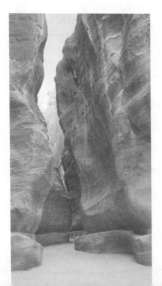

Reflection Questions

1 Read Numbers 20:2–13 and Exodus 17:1–7. How are
these stories similar and different? *Massah* means
"test" and *Meribah* means "quarrel." How does water
(or lack thereof) affect you and your actions? How
does God provide in such times?

_____

_____

_____

_____

_____

_____

_____

_____

_____

_____

_____

_____

_____

_____

2 Have you experienced a drought in your lifetime—physically or metaphorically? a flood? How did you react, and what did you learn in the aftermath?

_____

_____

_____

_____

_____

_____

_____

_____

_____

_____

_____

_____

_____

_____

_____

_____

3 What are the needs, hopes, and goals that need to be named on your financial spreadsheet?

_____

_____

_____

_____

_____

_____

4 How can you implement changes to insure a financial future that is prepared for any drought or flood that may occur in your future?

_____

_____

_____

_____

_____

_____

_____

_____

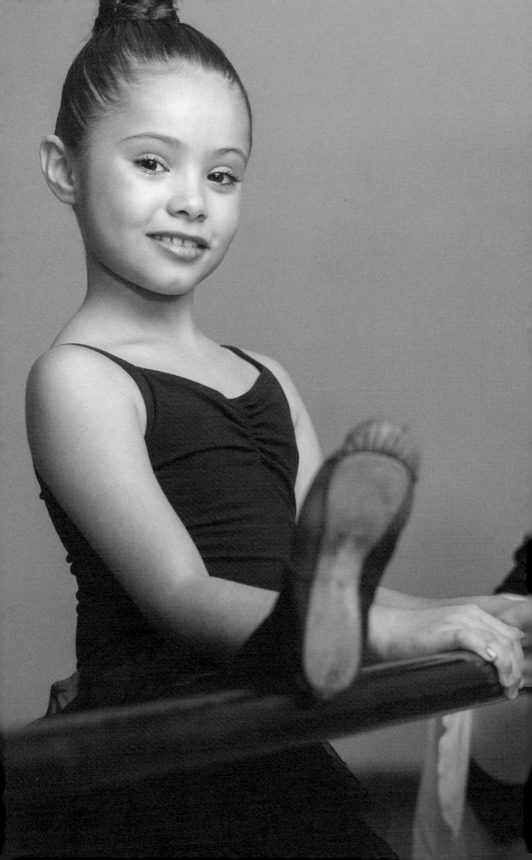

9

Ballet Barres, Balance, and Asset Allocation

I do not mean that there should be relief for others and pressure on you, but it is a question of a fair balance between your present abundance and their need, so that their abundance may be for your need, in order that there may be a fair balance.

2 Corinthians 8:13–14

My participation in ballet classes lasted for only a few of my elementary school years. It was great fun to be with friends and acting as if we were elegant and poised. I still remember the room, most of the positions (there are only five), and that darn ballet barre, the stationary rail designed to provide support. The ballet barre was not set well for me. I was three or four inches shorter than the other girls, and more than once, while I was trying to stretch way too high, my foot got caught. At times it could not even reach the ballet barre, which caused me to miss the next position; so much for poise.

> *The barre was a fixed object, not tailored to specific needs.*

The ballet barre threw me off from what it was created to help me do: balance. It was set into the wall at an average height and never seemed right for the tallest girl in class nor the shortest—me. The barre was a fixed object, not adjustable and not tailored to specific needs. Balance is essential to ballet, but without the flexibility of an adjustable barre, this young girl, moving on to middle school, dropped ballet in favor of tennis and surfing. Interestingly enough, each of these past-times requires balance; however, the tools for tennis and surfing can be tailored. My Hobie board was shaped for my skill and height, and my racquet's grip and weight fit my hands and strength.

Balance also has a vital place in the world of finance.

Balance also has a vital place in the world of finance. We use the phrase "asset allocation" to describe the balance of investments divided between stocks, bonds, and cash. I would like to encourage you—in fact I feel it is vitally important—to establish at least an annual intentional habit of review and, most likely, adjustment of your investments. The goal each year, or more often if major life changes occur, is to find your unique appropriate balance. Unlike the ballet barre height that I only wish could be adjusted to the height of the ballerina, asset allocation is best adjusted to an investor's needs, current holdings, earnings potential, risk tolerance, and ability to save. Another important factor is the direction of the economy. In other words, like the ballet barre, one-size-fits-all-at-all-times simply does not work.

How does one find their unique balance, their tailor-made asset allocation? For most of us, a financial advisor will guide us in the process; however, an advisor is not a substitute for basic understanding. The first step is to determine how your current investment assets are balanced: What is your anticipated retirement income and what are the sources of that income? What income flows in from "bond-like" Social Security and/or a Defined Benefit Pension? What portion of your future income is dependent on the growth of assets to at least slightly outpace inflation? Most of us are best balanced with a combination of fixed income and growth potential. What are your short-term, medium-term, and long-term needs and how well are they covered in your current asset allocation?

The second step is to increase your knowledge of basic economic principles. I like to use the image of a teeter-totter: upward pressure on one side forces the other side down. If interest rates are low, as they are now, at some time in the future—who knows when—interest rates will go higher. When interest rates rise due to inflation, the value of most existing bonds will go down. The stock market, especially stocks of companies with solid earnings, a view to the future, and a reasonable dividend—higher than today's money market rates—have provided, over many, many decades, a slight hedge against inflation.

Are your investments tailored and adjustable to your needs and your resiliency? Are you poised for what lies ahead? Are you teetering or balancing? ∾

ᖌᖇ Reflection Questions ᖇᖌ

1 Read 2 Corinthians 8:8–15. How would you express the principles of a fair balance in relation to Christ's generosity?

_____

_____

_____

_____

_____

_____

_____

_____

_____

_____

_____

_____

_____

_____

_____

2 Do you have a financial planner? If so, what questions might you have for him or her? If not, what steps do you need to take to find one you are comfortable with?

_____

_____

_____

_____

_____

_____

_____

3 How are your current investment assets balanced?

_____

_____

_____

_____

_____

_____

_____

_____

4 Do you have a retirement plan in place (financially)? Has it been updated to meet your current and future needs economically?

_____

_____

_____

_____

_____

_____

_____

_____

_____

_____

_____

_____

_____

_____

_____

_____

5 How are you poised for what lies ahead in your life?

_____

_____

_____

_____

_____

_____

_____

_____

_____

_____

_____

_____

_____

_____

_____

_____

_____

❧ 10 ❧

Values, Passions, and Structural Integrity

That one is like a man building a house, who dug deeply and laid the foundation on rock; when a flood arose, the river burst against that house but could not shake it, because it had been well built.

Luke 6:48

$\mathcal{M}$y dad was a mechanical, later turned aeronautical, engineer. Right out of college, he joined the Navy and was a Pacific Theatre Seabee, a member of a Construction Battalion. During World War II, the Seabees went wherever they were needed to build airstrips, bridges, and other necessary structures in anticipation of the presence of major air and troop activity. Structural integrity and soundness were essential in their work.

> *Structural integrity and soundness were essential in their work.*

In the mid-1970s through the late 1980s, our family tradition was to walk the Golden Gate Bridge on Christmas Day. In addition to the glorious 360-degree views, Dad would point out the structural components of the bridge and draw our attention to the ongoing work being done to maintain its physical integrity. Scaffolding was/is always here and there on the bridge, ready for workers who will be painting, stress testing, and doing repairs. Though decades have passed since our last family walk across the Golden Gate, I realized, while walking the bridge a few years back, that our conversations never addressed the underlying structure: the part mostly out of sight, the pillars and support coming up out of the headland waters of the Bay, and those anchoring the bridge to terra firma.

Financial planning is similar to maintaining a bridge. There is, every now and then, a need to pay attention to, and be involved with, the visible components: monitor budgets, work toward eliminating credit card debt, confirm insurance needs, save for retirement, explore college funding possibilities, and review investments and asset allocation. However, it's even more important to examine the integrity of the underlying structure, to do a stress test on the structure, the trellis, supporting your financial bridge.

Financial planning is similar to maintaining a bridge.

The Reverend Brian Taylor presents a five-part reflection in *Becoming Ourselves Again: Reclaiming Our Core Values*,[23] which offers useful material to explore, create, and/or revise one's core values and rule of life. Moreover, it can also serve as an excellent tool for assessing, establishing, and adjusting the structural integrity and soundness of pillars undergirding our financial plans.

The first of five sections explores "Passion and Principles." As Taylor states: Core values help ". . . direct us when we face a decision. They guide our ethics and fuel our passion for life. Unexamined, some strongly held values could also keep us stuck in unhealthy or self-limiting patterns and behaviors."[24] Two types of values are discussed: First, God's values, those that, as a result of our being made in God's image, we carry deep within. We only need to remember they are there and choose to tap into them. Second, we have values that come from our family, cultural money messages, our work environment, community and national tensions, and our unique passions. The image and purpose of a trellis again comes to mind. What pieces do you need to build a financial trellis? You might want to review chapter 1.

Can you name your core values?

Can you name your core values? If not, create some time and space to discover them. When you can name them, explore them. How did they come to be yours? How do they affect your handling, saving, spending, sharing, and investing of money? Are there value barnacles that have grown into colonies and are undermining your financial structure? Are the financial links to your deeply-held values strong, or are they in need of some reconstruction? Can you identify your passions and do they have a prominent role within your financial structure? Can you name the structural integrity and soundness of your financial plan? Do you know where your financial blueprints are and if so, are they in need of revision to increase sustainability? Are your core values weathering the storms and do they remain structurally sound? Where is your mooring? What is, or who is, holding you secure? ∾

↶ *Reflection Questions* ↷

1 Read Luke 6:46–49 and Matthew 7:24–27. Where do
you see complacency and misplaced security in these
teachings of Jesus? Where do you see them in your
own life?

2 What are your "God values" that you carry deep within yourself?

_____

_____

_____

_____

_____

_____

3 What are the values you have received from your family and other arenas of your life?

_____

_____

_____

_____

_____

_____

_____

_____

4 What are your core values about money?

_____

_____

_____

_____

_____

_____

_____

_____

_____

_____

_____

_____

_____

_____

_____

_____

_____

5 How secure do you feel about your finances? What could make you feel more stable and structurally sound?

_____

_____

_____

_____

_____

_____

_____

_____

_____

_____

_____

_____

_____

_____

_____

_____

_____

_____

∽ 11 ∽

Stork Nesting

*For everything there is a season,
and a time for every matter under heaven.*

Ecclesiastes 3:1

What comes to mind when you hear these words? Is it a big bird in a treetop nest or a description of something we do?

The first time I heard the phrase *stork nesting* was early in the summer of 2014 when it was wrapped into thrilling news that a baby would be born in January. Now every time the phrase comes to mind, I smile and feel a sense of joy of what is to be. In the meantime, family and friends wait and prepare.

> *Now every time the phrase comes to mind, I smile and feel a sense of joy of what is to be.*

One of the great gifts of attending a church, with institutions such as the Navy Postgraduate School and the Defense Language Institute close by, is the opportunity to get to know dedicated and delightful military families. They arrive, immerse themselves in activities and ministry for a year or two, hearts are touched, and then with both joy of what is to come and sadness for what will no longer be, depart for their next tour of duty. Such was the case with dear friends: mom, dad, and two daughters—the youngest of which is my goddaughter. They were here for less than a year, off to Italy, back to Monterey, off to D.C., and now in East Africa for up to two years. It was from East Africa that I heard of the one who is to come and the phrase *stork nesting* joined my lexicon.

So what is stork nesting? In the world of our military, it is what a pregnant woman does, beginning around thirty-four weeks, when local OB-GYN doctors, nurses, and delivery facilities are not available where they are stationed. She gets on a plane and flies to the closest regional medical center with stork nesting availability.[25] There she waits, prepares, and later joined by family, she and the one who is to come receive the care, nurture, and attention they need.

Liturgical seasons can be lenses through which we can clarify and come to a deeper understanding of many of the shifts in our lives.

When I first heard the phrase, I laughed. Quickly thereafter what came to mind were similarities with the liturgical seasons. Maybe it is because this particular family enters into a time of stork nesting during Advent, and then, sometime during Epiphany, their gift of new life was to be made palpable. Maybe, and more likely, it is that liturgical seasons can be lenses through which we can clarify and come to a deeper understanding of many of the shifts in our lives and transitions we experience. Advent, the time of preparation, of coming together, of renewing and receiving, and of celebrating, prepares us for Epiphany to see clearly a whole variety of gifts made manifest.

And yes, how we handle our finances can be seen through the lens of stork nesting. Here are the basics from the stork's point of view. They gather soft grasses, large twigs, and bare branches to use in building their nest. The nests are usually high atop a tree, a church spire, or the roof of a tall building. A stork's nest might be used for years. Both parents are actively involved in incubating the eggs, providing food for the chicks, and encouraging them to leave the nest. For us, financial nests are similar: preparation, wise usage, and at times, encouragement to leave the nest.

Financial nests are similar: preparation, wise usage, and at times, encouragement to leave the nest.

What are the nests you need to prepare? For some it might be college education: learning about the benefits of and how to establish a 529 College Savings Plan, funding those accounts on a regular basis, keeping them out of reach for regular day-in and day-out expenses, and spreading the word to family and friends that they are welcome to add soft grasses, twigs, and branches of any size.

For others it might be preparing for retirement decades before the actual event, after all our personal seasons of Advent, which are thankfully not limited to the four Sundays before Christmas. Have you explored whether the benefits of a tax-deferred retirement account such as a 403(b) or a 401(k) and/or an after-tax Roth IRA are best for you? Have the accounts been established and are they being funded on a regular basis? Are you, at least once a year, paying attention to your asset allocation? At times more soft grasses will be needed, and at other times large branches might best be emphasized.

Postscript: In January, on a clear winter night, an hour past midnight, Watson joined his loving family. Awaiting his parents, when they brought him home the next day, was an envelope with a contribution to his 529 College Saving Plan. I am immensely grateful for Watson's family's abundant capacity to give, receive, and share love. ℺

☜ Reflection Questions ☞

1 Read Ecclesiastes 3:1–8. Ecclesiastes is considered a wisdom book, and often reads as a philosophical treaty about life. It might be summarized with the question, "What does one gain by all one's toil?" How do the contrasting extremes in this passage relate to your view of life and your finances?

_____

_____

_____

_____

_____

_____

_____

_____

_____

_____

_____

_____

_____

2 When have you prepared for the coming of something new? How did you prepare? What new actions did you need to take?

_____

_____

_____

_____

_____

_____

_____

_____

_____

_____

_____

_____

_____

_____

_____

_____

3 What are the "financial nests" you need to prepare for in your future?

_____

_____

_____

_____

_____

_____

_____

_____

_____

_____

_____

_____

_____

_____

_____

_____

_____

_____

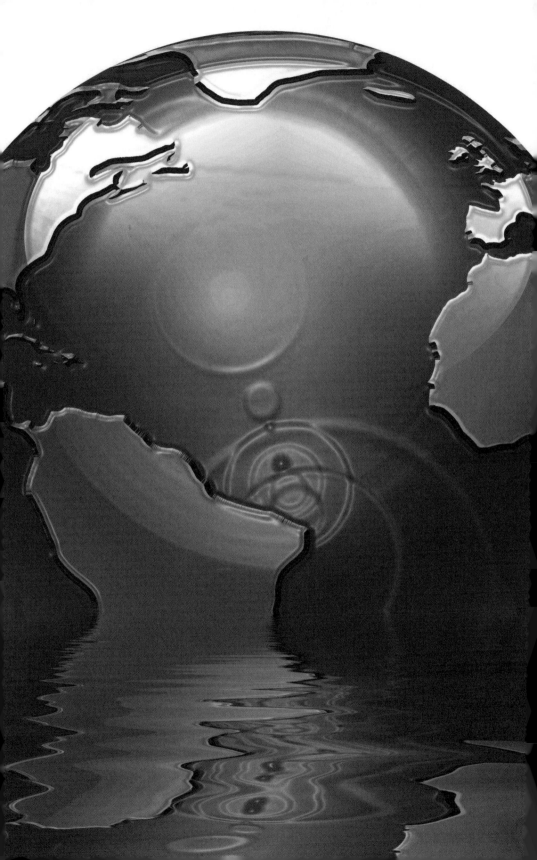

12

Reckless Generosity: Open Hands Full of Rich, Dark Chocolate

Mary took a pound of costly perfume made of pure nard, anointed Jesus's feet, and wiped them with her hair. The house was filled with the fragrance of the perfume.
John 12:3

God's light and life and love are there for us in abundance. It is a very sure tributary.

And it's there to be drawn on and given away with a kind of reckless generosity.
Brother Curtis Almquist[26]

It was the day after Ash Wednesday and a normal afternoon at the post office. After picking up the envelopes and catalogs in my P.O. Box, I, along with five other not-so-patient people, was waiting in line to get stamps and send packages. An elderly gentleman approached the line, and I realized I had seen him before. He looked, as he usually appeared, tired and a little disheveled.

He walked to the front of the line, which caused a few eyebrows to rise, and then he reached into his pocket, pulled out a fist full of something, and went down the line handing out small pieces of something. I looked closely as he placed one in my hand. It was foil-wrapped Dove™ chocolate—dark chocolate no less—and he wished each of us a Happy Valentine's Day.

Totally unexpected! He made my day and, from the delightful chatter in line, I know he made the day for the others. I am not sure whom among us might have given up chocolate for Lent—I had not—but I hope we all had the presence of mind to recognize and receive his gift for what it really was. In the parlance of Curtis Almquist, it was a gift of "reckless generosity."

> *The giver of chocolate was a symbol of Mary for me. It was as if he poured out costly perfume and let loose an unexpected scent of God in our midst.*

In many ways this gentleman reminded me of Mary, as in Mary and Martha of Bethany, when they welcomed Jesus into their home. Mary anointed Jesus' feet with costly perfume and nard. She was chastised for doing so as the perfume could have been sold and the money given to the poor. Jesus responds with "let her be." The giver of chocolate that day in the post office was a symbol of Mary for me. It was as if he poured out costly perfume and let loose an unexpected scent of God in our midst. And then he walked out and around the corner. I have not seen him since. His courageous audaciousness lingers with me like an herbal perfume and his open hands full of dark chocolate a metaphor of God's love. In many ways, Holy Week is an opportunity to focus on the reckless generosity, the steadfast love, the *chesed* of God.

May you this day, and the days to come, pray with eyes wide open, aware of the multitude of tributaries of God's reckless generosity. Let us, in all that needs to flow in our lives, not be the naysayer, but rather let us tap the inner Mary in each of us and be the lavish, impulsive sweet aroma of Christ . . . now and forever. ❧

❦ *Reflection Questions* ❦

1 Read John 12:1–8. What of great value can you offer to Christ? What is in your alabaster jar?

_____

_____

_____

_____

_____

_____

_____

_____

_____

_____

_____

_____

_____

_____

_____

_____

2 What are the gifts of reckless generosity you have received?

_____

_____

_____

_____

_____

_____

_____

_____

_____

_____

_____

_____

_____

_____

_____

_____

_____

_____

3 Have there been times when feasting and fasting intersect?

_____

_____

_____

_____

_____

_____

_____

_____

_____

_____

_____

_____

_____

_____

_____

_____

_____

_____

4 What tributary of God's love have you drawn from? And how can you, by giving away, share the abundance of the tributary with others?

_____

_____

_____

_____

_____

_____

_____

_____

_____

_____

_____

_____

_____

_____

_____

In Reflection

Whenever one contemplates, one necessarily at the same time contemplates in images.

Aristotle[27]

The Introduction invited you to complete the sentence: "The Kingdom of God is like . . . ." My hope is that you have made the time and created the means by which to wonder, ponder, and consider the underlining deep meaning and truth held by the images you associate with "The Kingdom of God." Have you named those images, drawn those images, and reflected on those images? Are your finances within or without the images? Does your handling of money reflect the Kingdom of God? What practices need to be disposed of, initiated, or refined? Who will you ask to walk alongside on this journey?

If you would like a flexible pathway as a guide to reflect on these questions, I have found a process of theological reflection, as designed by *Education for Ministry*,[28] one means by which reflection can be fruitful, insightful, and at times life changing. Using a modified process of TR (theological reflection), be open to what arises, go where your heart takes you, encounter God.

> *Does your handling of money reflect the Kingdom of God?*

❧ Meditate on the image to the left.

❧ What is the world like in this image? What is life like here?

- What can go wrong? Is there brokenness or separation?

- What catches you by surprise? What makes you do a double take, surprises, shocks, sheds light?

- What touches your heart, brings joy, and restores wholeness?

- What brings reconciliation, new life, redemption, and/or celebration?

- Do you experience the sacramental in this image?

- Does the image bring forth something within Scripture, prayer, blessing, or hymn? If so, name it and read, say, or sing it.

- Is there a connection to contemporary culture or a personal experience? If so, name those connections and remember some specifics.

- Where is God, through an aha, in the connection between this image and your experience?

- Although there might be a variety of implications and insights, see if there are some oriented toward your finances.

- Is there something about how the image connects your finances and your beliefs?

- Is there an affirmation, an insight, and/or a learning? What have you discovered?

- What are the financial implications for you, your family, friends, and greater community?

- What does the image say about your financial connections beyond your shores?

- What will you do with your insights and what difference will they make?

- How would you complete the sentence: "The Kingdom of God is like . . ."?

Now go and live it out.

Postscript: Photograph taken by Bishop Mary Gray-Reeves, on the Sea of Galilee/Lake Gennesaret, during a pilgrimage with her husband Michael, daughter Katie, and dear friends.

A Guide for Group Usage

We often do not discuss money and finances in our churches, except during "stewardship season" when congregations seek pledges from its members, during capital campaigns, or when preparing the annual budget. How might we engage in deeper conversation with one another as faithful Christians on the topic of money, understanding that how we handle our finances should also reflect our values?

Images found in agriculture and architecture and creation are some of the most universally understood. Jesus, in his use of the phrase ". . . it is like . . ." as well as with his metaphors and parables, intuitively knew the power of images. In this book, Celeste Ventura has explored images with the hope of an enhanced and increased engagement into how and why we earn, spend, invest, and share our money. Using the twelve images with corresponding reflection questions, we can build financial knowledge and engagement that can be transformational for our communities, the world, and us as individuals. ∾

Ways to Use this Book

1 The twelve images and reflections in this book can serve as a focus for a monthly, small group gathering for a year. Participants can read each chapter together followed by a discussion of the questions offered.

2 Use the text for a four- to six-week adult formation program (in Advent, Lent, or during your stewardship season).

3 Pair the reflections with guest speakers, such as a financial advisor, estate planner, tax accountant, college financial planner, legal advisor, and guests from charitable organizations. Be creative and also include a photographer and clergy person to offer an artistic and theological perspective about wholeness in our lives.

4 Invite participants to bring in their own images of financial wholeness to discuss and/or write about. Share these with the congregation. ∾

A Suggested Outline for a Program

1. Begin with Prayer

Almighty God, whose loving hand has given us all that we possess: Grant us grace that we may honor you with our substance, and, remembering the account which we must one day give, may be faithful stewards of your bounty, through Jesus Christ our Lord. Amen. (For the Right Use of God's Gifts, the Book of Common Prayer, p. 827)

2. Reflection Time

Invite one participant to read a chapter aloud while the group focuses on the image related to the chapter. Pause for silence after the reading.

3. Bible Study

Read the passage from Scripture (noted in Question #1 of each chapter) through once. Keep a few moments of silence. Read the passage again, with a new voice. Invite everyone to say a word or phrase that stands out for them. Read the passage a third time with a new voice. Share together what the word or phrase might mean and what questions it raises.

4. Discussion

Continue with any questions that are raised from the Bible study. Choose questions that are offered at the end of each chapter to go deeper in your conversation. Conclude by noting new learnings and what new steps individuals may be called to explore and act upon.

Deeper Simplicity, Broader Generosity

5. Conclusion

Close with the Lord's Prayer or another prayer of the group's choosing. ⟩⟨

Financial Concepts

529 College Plan. A plan operated by a state or educational institution, with tax advantages and potentially other incentives to make it easier to save for college and other post-secondary training for a designated beneficiary, such as a child or grandchild. Earnings are not subject to federal tax and generally not subject to state tax when used for the qualified education expenses of the designated beneficiary, such as tuition, fees, books, as well as room and board. Contributions to a 529 Plan, however, are not deductible.[29]

Asset Allocation. For those seeking to balance risk and reward, individual goals, and time horizons, asset allocation is a tool to allocate your investments among three main asset classes—equities, fixed income, and cash. Asset allocation is best reviewed with a financial advisor on an annual basis, or sooner if there are major changes in your goals and horizons.

Equities represent ownership in investments such as shares of stocks and mutual funds and Exchange Traded Funds (ETFs) with stock holdings. Fixed income represents, in basic terms, an IOU. The borrower promises to pay interest and return the original sum on a specific time schedule. This can be in the form of debt certificates such as corporate and municipal bonds, Treasuries, and Certificates of Deposit. Cash includes currency, savings accounts, money market accounts, and certificates with a year or less to maturity.

Cash Management. The practice of cash management includes understanding your sources and timing of income,
expenses, when bills need to be paid, regularity of savings
for emergency funds, college, medical needs, retirement,
and appropriate investing for now and the future. It
means budgeting and keeping on budget or tailoring the
budget, with both income and expenses, as needed. It
means understanding your financial needs, funding them,
and/or adapting as required.

Defined Benefit Pension. "In a defined benefit plan, an
employer commits to funding a plan that will result in the
employee receiving a benefit that is based on a formula
for life beginning at his or her retirement."[30] A pension
plan usually also provides ongoing benefits for a surviv-
ing beneficiary. The pension and benefits are based on a
formula using credited years of service and compensation.
It is not based on investment choices and market perfor-
mance.

Defined Contribution Plans. These are investment accounts that facilitate saving for your retirement. They are
usually "sponsored" for your employer, and the contribu-
tions/funding usually come from the employee. Employ-
ers may also make contributions, however that is not the
norm. The IRS sets a limit to annual contributions. The
most commonly known of these retirement accounts are
the 403(b) and the 401(k). The numbers refer to the loca-
tion of the explanations in the IRS Tax Code. The account
holder is responsible for the investment decisions; the
results, in contrast to a Defined Benefit Plan, do reflect
investment choices and market fluctuation.

Estate Planning. This practice is best when done with a blend of the pragmatic (process of developing and executing documents) as well as the conceptual. Estate planning includes documents such as Power of Attorney, wills, trusts, and advanced directives for medical care. It involves reflecting upon and naming an executor, maybe trustees, and someone to be a health advocate and, if necessary, exercise power of attorney for health matters. Parents will also name guardians for minor children in case of what we hope will never happen.

Generativity. "Coined by the psychoanalyst Erik Erikson in 1950 to denote a concern for establishing and guiding the next generation, it can be expressed in literally hundreds of ways, from raising a child to stopping a tradition of abuse, from writing a family history to restoring land. You try to 'make a difference' with your life, to 'give back,' to 'take care' of your community and your planet."[31]

Legacy. Although the legal world views legacy as something tangible, legacy can also be expressed intangibly, passed either intentionally or unintentionally, from one generation to another in the form of beliefs and values, forgiveness given, forgiveness received, experiences shared, memories made, and stories told. To understand how we deal with finances has been formed through and reflects the intersection of people and events from past generations, events and values of our immediate family, and models of financial integrity.

Money Messages. Money message are myths, which may or may not contain the truth, about money. They are messages we heard as we grew up, and often they affect the way we deal with money issues later in life. For example, you might have heard, "Money doesn't grow on trees," or "Money can't buy happiness," or "It's better to give than to receive." Understanding not only your family experiences around money, but also how those money messages affect your handling of money today, is the cornerstone of putting your financial values into perspective.

Risk Tolerance. Understanding your tolerance for risk is a vital element in investing. There are a variety of risk tolerance questionnaires to assist individuals in determining their risk tolerance. These will guide you through an exploration of your time horizon, your level of emergency funds, and your ability to sleep at night when the markets are volatile.

A Rule of Life. The Northumbrian Community states: ". . . a Rule of Life points the way to 'this is who we are, this is our story'; and it reminds us of those things God has put on our hearts, calling us back to our foundations. The idea of a Rule of Life developed in Christian monastic communities, and indeed, monasteries and convents today still function under a Rule, the best known of which is that of St. Benedict, dating from the sixth century."[32] There is, however, no rule that one must be a monastic in order to have a Rule of Life. Develop your own, tweak it as life happens, live into it, and journey toward making your "Rule" visible in how you handle a variety of aspects of daily living, including your finances. ∾

Annotated Bibliography

Deedy, Carmen and Gonzales, Thomas. *14 Cows for America*. Peachtree Publishers: 2009.

This is one of those fabulous "children's books" that speaks deeply to the hearts of young and old alike. In light of 9/11, Kimeli, a young Maasai, did what is deeply embedded in Maasai culture: To "heal a sorrowing heart, we must give something dear to our hearts."

Palmer, Parker J. *A Hidden Wholeness: The Journey Toward An Undivided Life*. Jossey-Bass: 2004.

Dr. Palmer, by focusing on integrity not as moral rightness but rather as wholeness, encourages us to live an undivided life. From deep within his Quaker practice comes the wisdom of "reaching in toward wholeness, reaching out toward the world's need, and trying to live lives at the intersection of the two."

Wolfe, Linnie Marsh. *John of the Mountains: The Unpublished Journals of John Muir*. University of Wisconsin Press: 1979.

Although money is rarely mentioned, wisdom, easily converted to the multitude of facets of our lives, emanates from experiencing nature first hand. As John Muir said in *My First Summer in the Sierra,* "When one tugs at a single thing in nature, he finds it attached to the rest of the world."

Zevit, Rabbi Shawn Israel. *Offerings of the Heart: Money and Values in Faith Communities.* The Alban Institute: 2005.

"A deep understanding of generosity and giving is brought to bear on the practicalities of budgets, planning, and reaching out in deeds of justice and mercy." The Rev. Loren B. Mead

Kinder, George. *Seven Stages of Money Maturity.* Dell: 2000.

How often have you thought about blending Buddhist wisdom with your handling of money? George Kinder, poet, photographer, financial advisor, and Buddhist practitioner, does just that. The effect is surprisingly wonderful.

Williams, Rosemary. *A Woman's Book of Money & Spiritual Vision.* Innisfree Press: 2001.

The title is a little misleading. The content would lead me to entitle it "A Book of Money and Spiritual Vision." The author's words remind us—woman or man—there is no reason to hold money separate from spirituality. Please integrate the two.

For specific financial planning resources, retirement planning tools, and insurance calculators, please consult your financial advisor, your denominational pension organization, and/or any well-respected financial firm or online site. ❧

Notes

1. Desmond Tutu. www.huffingtonpost.com/sean-jacobs/des-mond-tutu-compares-oba_b_143065.html (Accessed February 6, 2015).

2. Aristotle (384–322 BCE). De Anima iii 8, 432a8–9, 431a16–17; De Memoria 1, 449b31–450a1.

3. Douglas Wood, Fawn Island (Minneapolis: University of Minneapolis Press, 2001), 3–4.

4. Parker Palmer, A Hidden Wholeness: The Journey Toward an Undivided Life (San Francisco: Jossey-Bass, 2004), 3.

5. John Donne, No Man is An Island, Meditation XVII (1624).

6. Palmer, 5.

7. Ibid., 5.

8. Wood, 4.

9. http://childdevelopmentinfo.com/child-development/er-ickson/#ixzz3QiqzZLUO (Accessed February 3, 2015).

10. http://14cowsforamerica.com

11. www.nytimes.com/2009/11/08/books/review/Kristof-t.html?nl=books&emc=booksupdateemb2&_r=1& (Accessed January 9, 2015).

12. Carmen Agra Deedy, 14 Cows for America (Atlanta: Peachtree Publishers, 2009), 29.

13. Thomas Merton, "ELIAS—Variations on a Theme" in The Strange Islands (New Directions, 1957). http://louielouietwo.wordpress.com/2007/08/03/hello-world/ (Accessed February 6, 2015).

14. Here is one example: www.lifehappens.org/insurance-over-view/life-insurance/calculate-your-needs/ (Accessed February 6, 2015).